The Magic School Bus

Explores the Senses

S
EE
HEAR
SMELL TASTE
TOUCH

The Magic School Bus
Explores the Senses

By Joanna Cole
Illustrated by Bruce Degen

Scholastic Press / New York

For his careful reading of the manuscript and illustrations, we thank Bruce Rideout, Ph.D.,
Professor of Behavioral Neuroscience, Ursinus College. His untiring attention to the details
helped us enormously. Thanks also to David A. Stevens, Ph.D.; Matthew D. Paul, M.D.;
Brian J. Silverlieb, V.M.D.; Lorraine Hopping Egan; Karen Pierce;
and, as always, Stephanie Calmenson.

Library of Congress Cataloging-in-Publication Data
Cole, Joanna
The magic school bus explores the senses /
by Joanna Cole; illustrated by Bruce Degen.   p.   cm.
Summary: Ms. Frizzle and her class explore the senses by traveling on the magic school bus
in and out of an eye, ear, mouth, nose, and other parts of both human and animal bodies.
ISBN 0-590-44697-5
1. Senses and sensation — Juvenile literature.
[1. Senses and sensation.] I. Degen, Bruce, ill. II. Title.
QP434.C565   1999   612.8 — dc21   98-18662
CIP   AC

10 9 8 7 6 5 4 3 2 1   9/9 0/0 01 02 03 04

Printed in the U.S.A.   36
First edition, March 1999

The text type was set in 15 point Bookman Light.
The illustrator used pen and ink, watercolor, color pencil,
and gouache for the paintings in this book.

For David Hashmall, whose friendly wisdom
and guidance always make perfect *sense!*
— J.C. & B.D.

WITHOUT OUR SENSES,
WE'D BE OUT OF IT
                by Carlos
  If someone could not
see, hear, feel, taste, or
smell, that person
would not be able to
tell any thing about the
outside world.

Our class was studying the senses —
how people and animals know
what's going on around them.
We were doing experiments and writing reports.
We were even learning a song about the senses
to sing at an important parent-teacher meeting.
The day before the meeting, we practiced our
song twenty times.

HEAR A SCHOOL BELL RING,
SEE A BRIGHT LIGHT SHINE,
TOUCH A CAT'S SOFT FUR,
YOU'LL BE JUST IN TIME...

TO COME TO YOUR
SENSES!

SEE

TASTE

TOUCH

SMELL

HEAR

6

It would have been easier if we had an ordinary teacher.
But we don't — we have Ms. Frizzle.
Looking at her dress made us forget the tune.
Her shoes made us forget the words.
And her wacky personality made us forget
almost everything else!

CLASS, THE SHOW IS TOMORROW EVENING.

TASTE A SCHOOL BELL RING...

SMELL A BRIGHT LIGHT SHINE...

SOMEHOW, I DON'T THINK WE'LL BE READY....

My favorite smell by Phoebe

EVERY ANIMAL NEEDS SENSES
by Arnold
Without senses, an animal could not find food or escape from danger.

I SEE YOU! I HEAR YOU! I SMELL YOU!

I SEE, HEAR, AND SMELL YOU, TOO!

EVEN THE TINIEST ANIMALS HAVE SENSES
by Keesha
One-celled animals have simple senses. They can tell when their surroundings are too hot, too cold, or too poisonous.
Then they turn around and go the other way!

I MAY BE MICROSCOPIC, BUT I'M SENSITIVE!

7

WHICH SENSES ARE MOST IMPORTANT?
by Phil

Different kinds of animals rely on different senses.

Seeing is most important to birds. They can't find food if they can't see it!

Bats use <u>hearing</u> to tell them where they're going. They can't hunt if their ears are blocked.

Snakes <u>smell</u> the air with their forked tongues. If a snake's tongue isn't working, it's hard for it to find its prey.

THAT SMELLS YUMMY!

8

When the school day was over,
we went outside to warm up for a game.
After a while, Ms. Frizzle came out and got in her car.
At the same moment, Mr. Wilde,
our new assistant principal, called to us,
"See you at the meeting tonight."
"Tonight!?" we groaned. "Ms. Frizzle thinks it's tomorrow!"
"I have to tell her," said Mr. Wilde.
But it was too late. The Friz was already driving away.

MR. WILDE IS A GREAT ASSISTANT PRINCIPAL, BUT I DON'T THINK HE CAN HANDLE THE BUS....

HE DOES SEEM LIKE A QUIET SORT OF GUY.

HE NEEDS OUR HELP!

LET'S GO!

"I've got to catch up with Ms. Frizzle!" said Mr. Wilde.
To our surprise, he got behind the wheel of our bus.
Believe us, we've had a lot of experience with that bus.
We couldn't let Mr. Wilde drive it. Not all by himself!
After all, he's only an assistant principal —
he's not Ms. Frizzle!
We all jumped on board.

OUR TOP SENSES
by Wanda
Seeing and hearing
are the two most
important senses
for humans.

STOP! LOOK! LISTEN!

COME BACK, MS. FRIZZLE!

WALKERVILLE ELEMENTARY

STOP

CROSSING GUARD

FRIZ

As Ms. Frizzle went faster,
some papers blew out of her car.
They were her Teacher's Notes about the senses.
They came flying in the windows of our bus,
and we saved them for her.
Mr. Wilde drove carefully out of the parking lot.
We were only a few cars behind the Friz.
We would catch up to her in no time.

Then Mr. Wilde saw a little green switch on the dashboard.
"Green means go," he muttered to himself,
reaching for the switch.
"DON'T TOUCH IT!" we warned.
But it was too late. Mr. Wilde flipped the switch.
He had never been in a school bus like this one before.
But we had — plenty of times.
We knew that something impossible was going to happen.
And it did. The bus began to shrink.

WHAT MAKES YOUR EYES MOVE?
by Florrie
There are six muscles attached to each of your eyeballs.

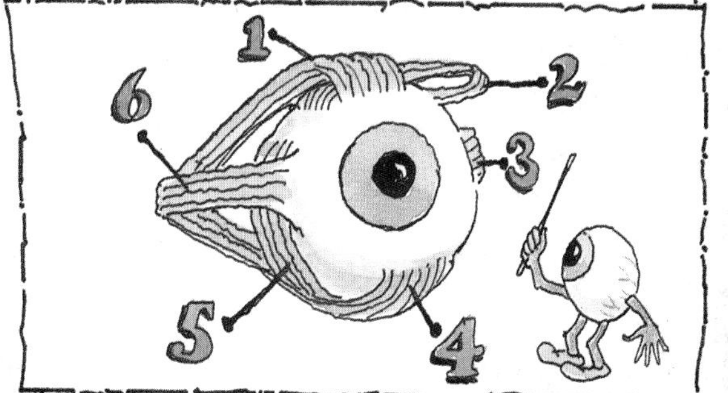

They move the eyes in different directions.

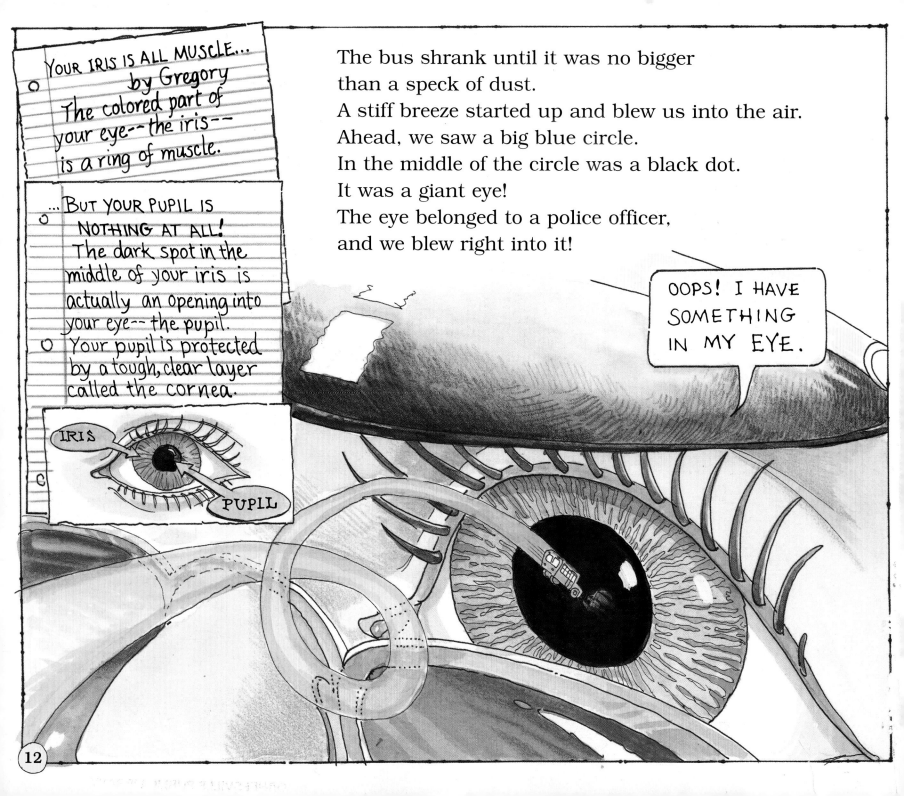

YOUR IRIS IS ALL MUSCLE...
by Gregory
The colored part of your eye-- the iris-- is a ring of muscle.

...BUT YOUR PUPIL IS NOTHING AT ALL! The dark spot in the middle of your iris is actually an opening into your eye-- the pupil. Your pupil is protected by a tough, clear layer called the cornea.

IRIS

PUPIL

The bus shrank until it was no bigger
than a speck of dust.
A stiff breeze started up and blew us into the air.
Ahead, we saw a big blue circle.
In the middle of the circle was a black dot.
It was a giant eye!
The eye belonged to a police officer,
and we blew right into it!

OOPS! I HAVE SOMETHING IN MY EYE.

Before the officer could blink us out,
Mr. Wilde saw a rainbow-colored lever.
"LEAVE THE LEVER ALONE!" we yelled.
But he couldn't resist. He pulled the lever,
and the bus slid smoothly through the cornea —
the clear covering that protects the iris and the pupil.
Beyond the cornea, we passed through a sea of
clear liquid ... past the blue iris ... and through the pupil.
"Who knew driving a bus was so much fun?"
asked Mr. Wilde.

BROWN   BLACK   BLUE   HAZEL   GREEN   GRAY

IRIS

CORNEA

PUPIL

IRIS

I'M DRIVING INTO AN EYE?? I CAN'T BELIEVE IT, PHOEBE!

AT MY OLD SCHOOL PUPILS NEVER WENT INTO A PUPIL!

MY CLASS IS REALLY INTO THE HUMAN EYE.

THEY'D BETTER LOOK OUT!

MOM'S SPRING WATER COLD AND PURE... JUST LIKE MOM USED TO SERVE.

FRIZZLE FACT
When the muscles of the iris tighten, the pupil gets smaller. Then less light enters your eye. When the muscles relax, the pupil gets larger. More light gets in.
TRY THIS AND SEE:
YOUR PUPILS GET SMALLER IN BRIGHT LIGHT...
...AND BIGGER IN DIM LIGHT.

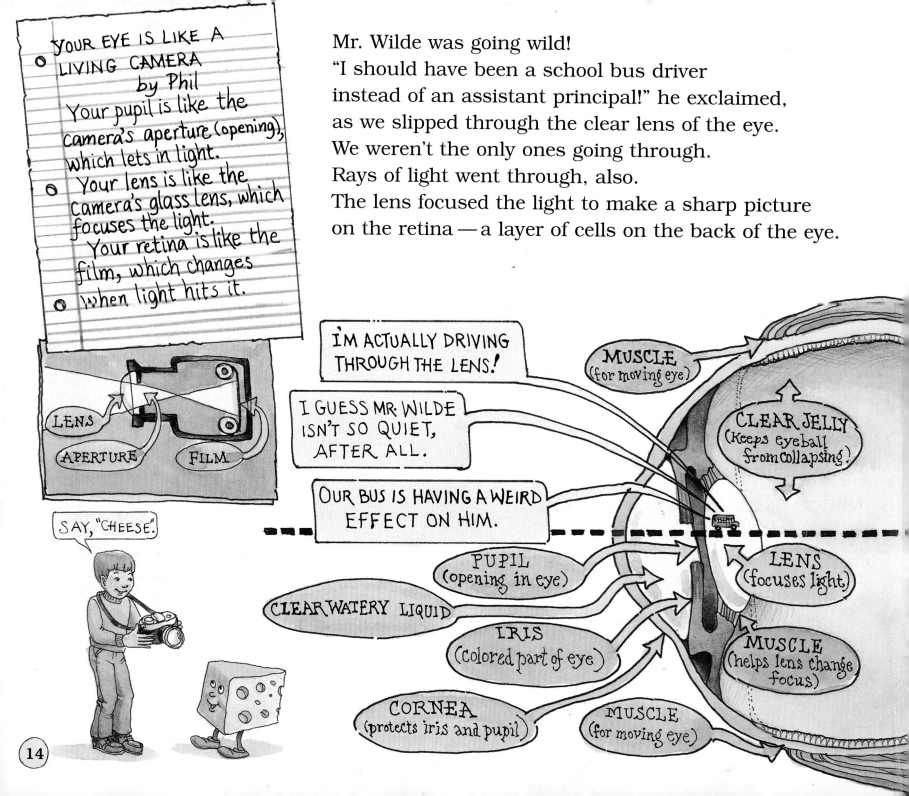

Mr. Wilde was going wild!
"I should have been a school bus driver
instead of an assistant principal!" he exclaimed,
as we slipped through the clear lens of the eye.
We weren't the only ones going through.
Rays of light went through, also.
The lens focused the light to make a sharp picture
on the retina — a layer of cells on the back of the eye.

"Let's go to the retina," said Mr. Wilde,
gunning the engine.
There was no stopping him now!
The Teacher's Notes said the retina is made up of
special cells called rods and cones.
These cells change the light that falls on them.
The pattern of light becomes a pattern
of nerve signals going to the brain.
"It's like translating one language into another," said Tim.
"The rods and cones translate
'light language' into 'nerve language.'"

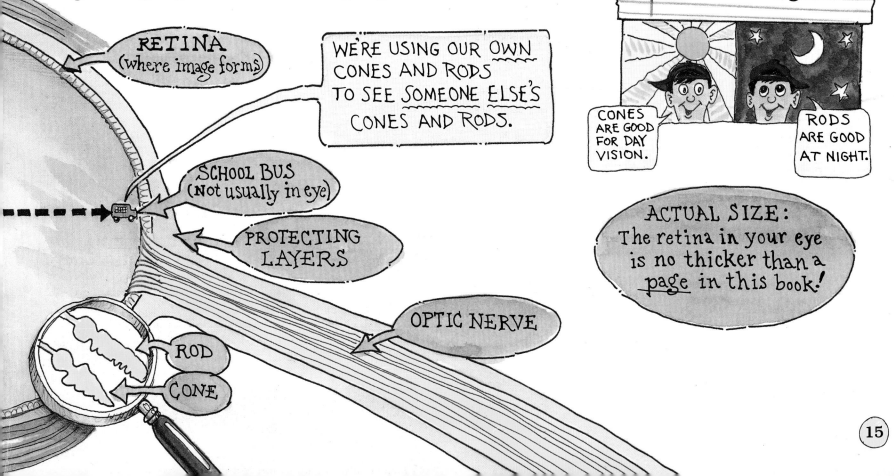

RODS AND CONES:
WHAT'S THE DIFFERENCE?
by Ralphie

We need both rods and cones for good vision. **Cone cells** let us see clearly and in color. They work best in bright light. When we use **rod cells** our vision is blurry and we cannot see colors.

However, we need rods to see in dim light.

RETINA
(where image forms)

WE'RE USING OUR OWN CONES AND RODS TO SEE SOMEONE ELSE'S CONES AND RODS.

CONES ARE GOOD FOR DAY VISION.

RODS ARE GOOD AT NIGHT.

SCHOOL BUS
(Not usually in eye)

PROTECTING LAYERS

ACTUAL SIZE:
The retina in your eye is no thicker than a page in this book!

OPTIC NERVE

ROD

CONE

Mr. Wilde had forgotten all about
delivering his message to the Friz.
All he cared about was driving the bus.
All we cared about was finding Ms. Frizzle.
Keesha flipped through the Teacher's Notes,
trying to figure out where we were.
"Look! Here's a map of the retina," she said.
"'The spot in the center of the retina is the fovea.
That's the part of the eye we use when we
look directly at something.'"

"What's the other round spot on the retina?" we asked.
"It's called the blind spot," answered Keesha.
Everyone is blind in that little spot of the eye.
It's where all the nerves in the eye come together.
They form a bundle called the optic nerve,
which runs from the eye to the brain."
A smile spread over Mr. Wilde's face
as he steered the bus into the optic nerve.

WHY CAN'T THE
BLIND SPOT "SEE"?
by Keesha
Because there are no
rods or cones on that
spot.

MAKE MS. FRIZZLE'S
SHOE DISAPPEAR!

HOW TO DO IT:
• Hold this book at arm's
length in front of your face.
• Cover your right eye.
• Look at the ✗ with your
left eye.
• Move the book slowly toward
your face, and then away
again.
• When the shoe disappears,
stop.
• The image of the shoe is
right on your blind spot.

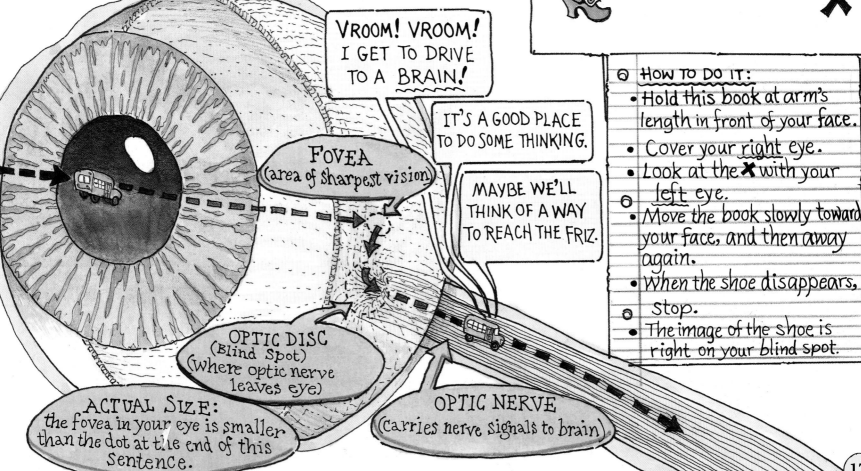

VROOM! VROOM!
I GET TO DRIVE
TO A BRAIN!

IT'S A GOOD PLACE
TO DO SOME THINKING.

MAYBE WE'LL
THINK OF A WAY
TO REACH THE FRIZ.

FOVEA
(area of sharpest vision)

OPTIC DISC
(Blind Spot)
(where optic nerve
leaves eye)

ACTUAL SIZE:
the fovea in your eye is smaller
than the dot at the end of this
sentence.

OPTIC NERVE
(carries nerve signals to brain)

17

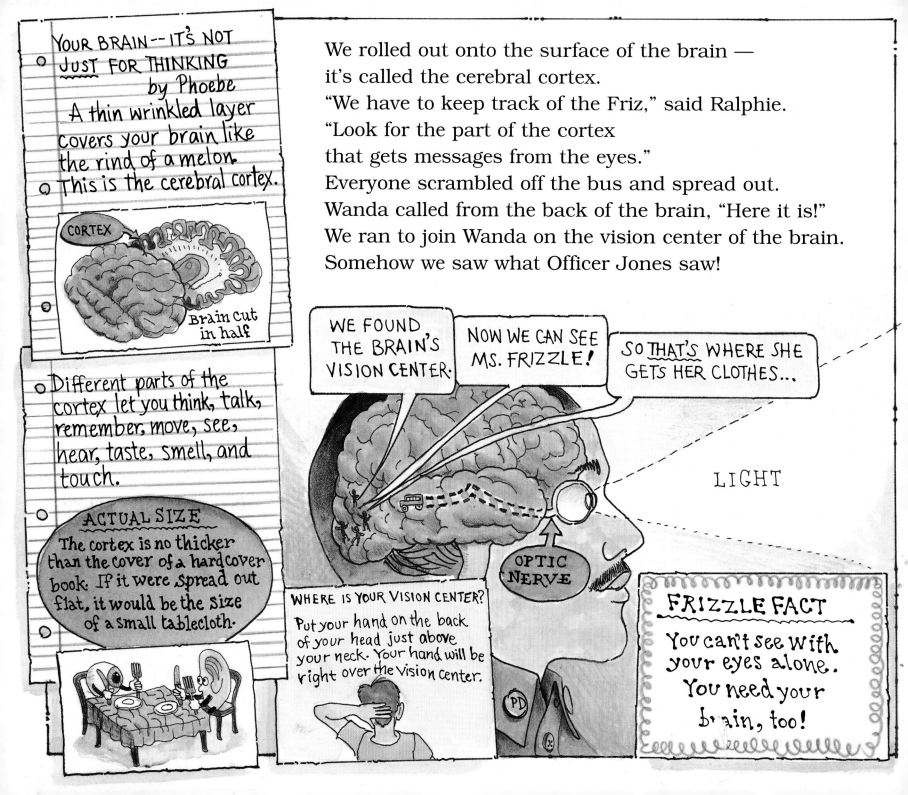

YOUR BRAIN -- IT'S NOT JUST FOR THINKING
by Phoebe

A thin wrinkled layer covers your brain like the rind of a melon. This is the cerebral cortex.

CORTEX

Brain cut in half

Different parts of the cortex let you think, talk, remember, move, see, hear, taste, smell, and touch.

ACTUAL SIZE
The cortex is no thicker than the cover of a hardcover book. If it were spread out flat, it would be the size of a small tablecloth.

We rolled out onto the surface of the brain — it's called the cerebral cortex.
"We have to keep track of the Friz," said Ralphie.
"Look for the part of the cortex that gets messages from the eyes."
Everyone scrambled off the bus and spread out.
Wanda called from the back of the brain, "Here it is!"
We ran to join Wanda on the vision center of the brain.
Somehow we saw what Officer Jones saw!

WE FOUND THE BRAIN'S VISION CENTER.

NOW WE CAN SEE MS. FRIZZLE!

SO THAT'S WHERE SHE GETS HER CLOTHES...

LIGHT

OPTIC NERVE

WHERE IS YOUR VISION CENTER?
Put your hand on the back of your head just above your neck. Your hand will be right over the vision center.

FRIZZLE FACT
You can't see with your eyes alone. You need your brain, too!

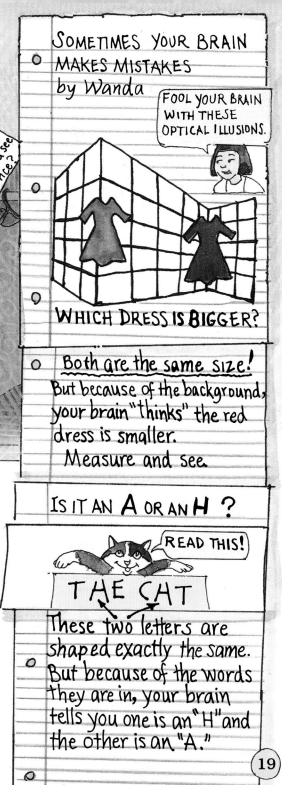

There was Ms. Frizzle in a dress shop,
buying a dress with optical illusions on it.
We called for help, but of course she couldn't hear us.
She didn't know that Mr. Wilde was driving the bus.
She didn't know that her class was in a brain.
She didn't know that everything was totally out of control.
And we couldn't tell her!

LOOK AT YOUR EARS
by Alex

The part you can see is called the auricle, or pinna. It has no bones. Inside the auricle is a tough, bendable material called cartilage.

The opening in the ear leads to the ear canal.

Together, the auricle and the ear canal make up your outer ear.

THERE'S MORE TO YOUR EAR THAN MEETS THE EYE!
by Amanda Jane

Most of your ear is deep inside your head. You can't see it.

EAR CANAL
AURICLE
OUTER EAR
INNER EAR

Then we felt something rumbling.
Officer Jones was on his motorcycle, riding away!
We had to stay close to the Friz.
We jumped on the bus, and Mr Wilde swerved back onto the path of nerves that led to the eye.
Our bus teetered on the edge of the eyelid, then dropped through the eyelashes!
When we looked down, we saw an EAR!

WE HAVE TO GET OUT OF HERE!

WE HAVE TO GET CLOSER TO THE FRIZ!

WE HAVE TO GET ACCIDENT INSURANCE!

LOOK AT ME! NO HANDS!

WHAT ARE SOUND WAVES?
by Tim
When something moves back and forth rapidly, the air around it moves, too. These movements are sound waves, or vibrations.

WHEN A BELL RINGS
by Rachel
1. Clapper hits bell.
2. Bell vibrates.
3. Sound waves go through air.
4. Waves enter your ear.
5. Your hearing system starts to work.
6. You hear the bell ring!

At the end of the ear canal, we hit
a thin, stretchy membrane called the eardrum.
We came tumbling out of the bus
just as some sound waves entered the ear.
They made the eardrum vibrate.
We vibrated right along — through the eardrum
and into the middle ear. So did our bus.

EARDRUMS SURE ARE BOUNCY.

THAT MUST MAKE THEM VIBRATE BETTER.

JUST LIKE REAL DRUMS.

LET'S GO, RICHIE

FRIZZLE WARNING
Take care of your drums! Never put anything in your ear... especially not a busload of children!

There was nothing in the middle ear
except air and three ossicles —
small bones that carry sound vibrations.
Sound waves traveled from one bone to the next.
We went, too, and the bus rolled behind us.

I'M CLIMBING GIANT BONES!

THESE OSSICLES SEEM BIG TO US BUT...

THEY ARE ACTUALLY THE SMALLEST BONES IN THE HUMAN BODY.

WE'RE ACTUALLY THE SMALLEST HUMAN BODIES IN THESE BONES.

HAMMER

EARDRUM

ANVIL

STIRRUP

A WORD FROM DOROTHY ANN
Ossicle comes from a word that means "little bone."

NAME THAT BONE!
by Molly
Your three ossicles are called:
Anvil
Hammer
Stirrup
They have these names because they look a bit like these objects.

ACTUAL SIZE
The stirrup, the smallest ossicle, is smaller than a grain of rice.

23

Then we came to another stretchy membrane.
This one was called the oval window.
The last ossicle, the stirrup, was resting right on top of it.
Dorothy Ann read from Ms. Frizzle's notes, "Children, the oval window separates the middle ear from the inner ear."
"Inner ear, here we come!" shouted Wanda, as we went through.
We were going to the inner ear — whether we liked it or not!

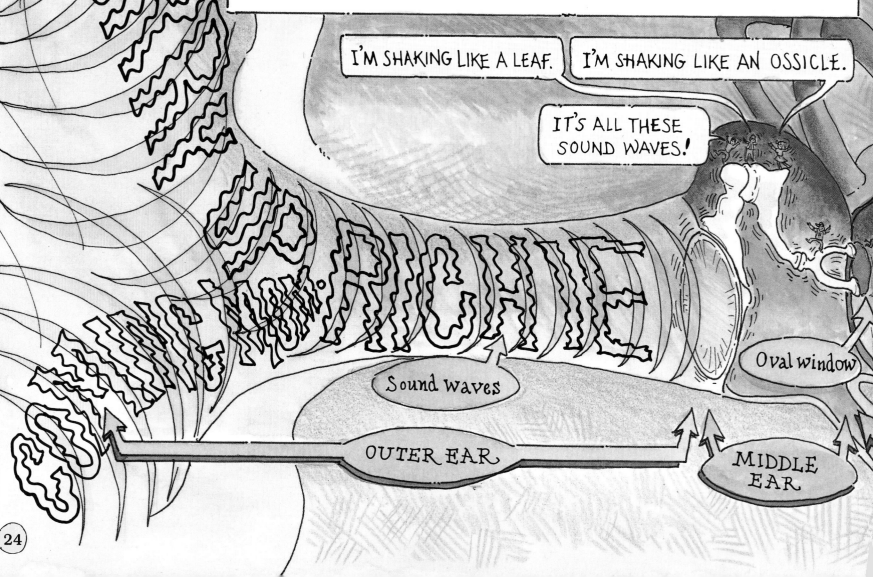

So far, all the parts of the ear had only one job —
to *carry* vibrations.
In the inner ear, we saw the part that
receives vibrations — the cochlea.
We swam through the liquid inside the cochlea.
We saw cells that looked like tiny hairs.
Ms. Frizzle's notes said, "Hair cells are sound receptors.
They translate sound vibrations into nerve signals."
As soon as we were on the bus again, Mr. Wilde
followed the nerve signals along the auditory nerve.

CAN YOU COMB YOUR HAIR CELLS?
by John
No! Hair cells aren't really hairs. They just look like them.

The hair cells in your ear have the same kind of job as the cones and rods in your eye.
Both kinds of cells take in a form of energy-- either light or sound waves-- and change it into nerve signals.

WOW! I GET TO DRIVE INTO THE BRAIN TWICE!

ONCE WAS NOT ENOUGH?

AUDITORY NERVE
(Carries signals to the brain)

INNER EAR

FRIZZLE WARNING
Very loud noises can damage the hair cells in your inner ears.

THIS INCLUDES LOUD MUSIC! TURN DOWN THE VOLUME!

ANOTHER WORD FROM DOROTHY ANN
Cochlea comes from a word that means "Snail."
The cochlea in your ear looks like a snail shell.

COCHLEA
SNAIL
D.A. IN A SNAIL COSTUME

This time, we went to a different part of the cortex —
the hearing center for the ear we were in.
As soon as we were standing on it,
we could somehow hear what the little kid heard.
It was Ms. Frizzle reading from her "Things-to-Do" list.
She was nearby! Maybe there was still hope.
Maybe the Friz could rescue us!

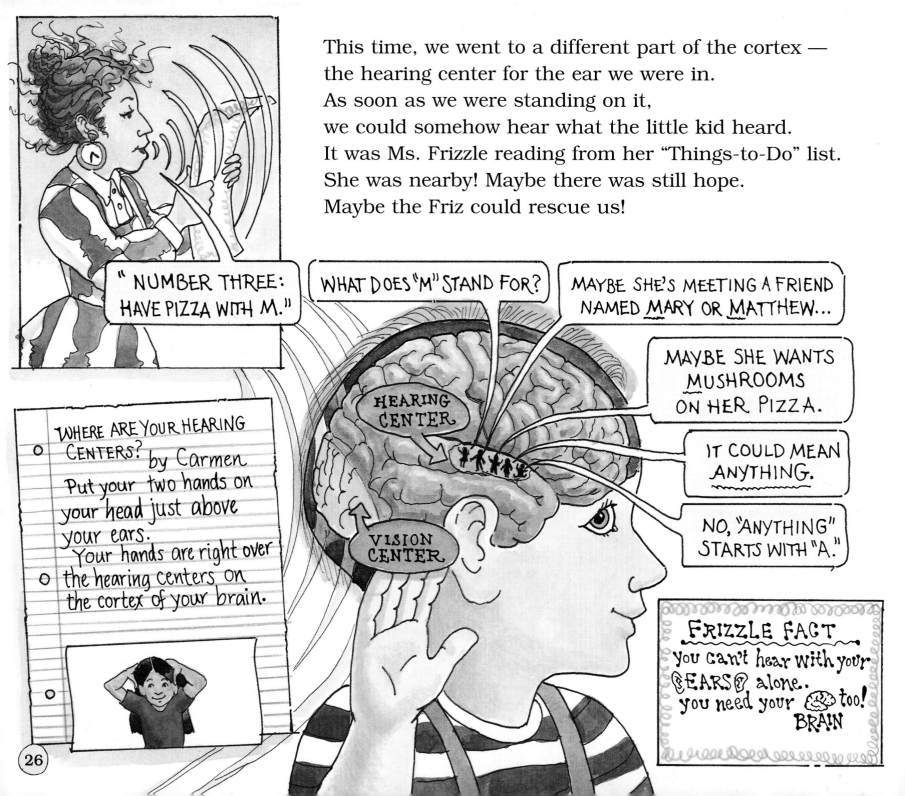

"NUMBER THREE: HAVE PIZZA WITH M."

WHAT DOES "M" STAND FOR?

MAYBE SHE'S MEETING A FRIEND NAMED MARY OR MATTHEW...

MAYBE SHE WANTS MUSHROOMS ON HER PIZZA.

IT COULD MEAN ANYTHING.

NO, "ANYTHING" STARTS WITH "A."

HEARING CENTER

VISION CENTER

WHERE ARE YOUR HEARING CENTERS? by Carmen
Put your two hands on your head just above your ears.
Your hands are right over the hearing centers on the cortex of your brain.

FRIZZLE FACT
you can't hear with your EARS alone.
you need your BRAIN too!

Then we heard heels clicking on the sidewalk.
They were Ms. Frizzle's heels! She was walking away!
We had to follow her, so we ran for the bus.
We sped over the brain, into the auditory nerve,
through the ear, and out the ear canal.
Then we started falling!

WHEE! I'M SKY-DIVING!

DON'T YOU NEED A PARACHUTE FOR THAT?

MS. FRIZZLE, WAIT FOR US!

WE NEED HELP!

I DON'T THINK SHE CAN HEAR US.

Now HEAR THIS!
by Florrie
Crickets have their eardrums on their legs.

Mosquitoes can hear with their antennae.

Snakes have no ears. They pick up sound through their bones.

I SURE AM HUNGRY!

27

This time there was no soft ear to catch us.
We saw the hard sidewalk rushing up at us!
Then, just before our bus crashed,
something amazing happened.
A friendly dog, smelling her way along Main Street,
snuffed us up.

IT'S A LONG WAY DOWN.

NOT LONG ENOUGH...
WE'RE GOING TO CRASH!

SOON!

NOW!

SNORF

"What? Another
Series?" - N.Y. Times
"CHILDISH!"
- The New Yorker

ARTY MAGAZINE
"DEGEN SHOWS HIS
ARTWORK"...

HOW WE SEE
by
Rod N. COHEN

TEST YOUR HEARING
by LOUDEN KLEER

Your pet Skunk
by Holden D. Nose

Sensitive Skin
by Hans Orff

TASTEFUL TOPICS
by
SWEDEN SOUR

SENSIBLE
BOOKS
AT OVER 5 LOCATIONS

At first we were happy because we were safe.
Then the full impact of our situation hit us.
We were inside a dog's nose!

THIS IS A NIGHTMARE!

IT'S SLIMY, TOO.

WE'LL NEVER FIND MS. FRIZZLE NOW!

WISDOM from the FRIZ-DOM
Never say never!

DOGS ARE SUPER SMELLERS
by Arnold
Dogs can smell odors that are very, very faint or very, very far away. Bloodhounds can tell one person from another just from the scent that comes through their shoes.

...AND IT'S TIME TO CHANGE YOUR SOCKS!

MY STUDENTS HAVE A NOSE FOR ADVENTURE.

NOT ME!

29

Mr. Wilde drove to one of the smell areas. Then we could smell what the dog smelled. It was easy to tell when we were close to the pizza restaurant!

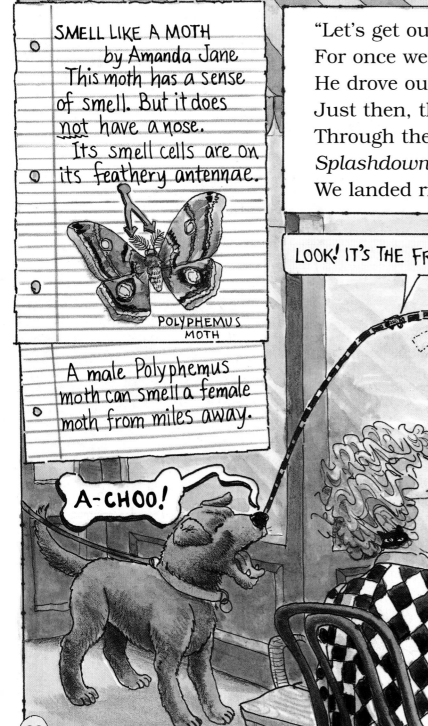

SMELL LIKE A MOTH
     by Amanda Jane
This moth has a sense of smell. But it does not have a nose.
     Its smell cells are on its feathery antennae.

POLYPHEMUS MOTH

A male Polyphemus moth can smell a female moth from miles away.

"Let's get out and have some pizza," said Mr. Wilde.
For once we all approved of his plan.
He drove out of the brain and back to the nose.
Just then, the dog sneezed and the bus flew out.
Through the windows we saw the Friz sitting at a table.
Splashdown!
We landed right in her water glass!

The bus got a good washing — it needed one!
Then a waiter accidently knocked over the glass.
We were tossed onto Ms. Frizzle's pizza!
Mr. Wilde tried to get away, but the pizza had extra cheese.
While we were spinning our wheels, the Friz decided to take a bite!

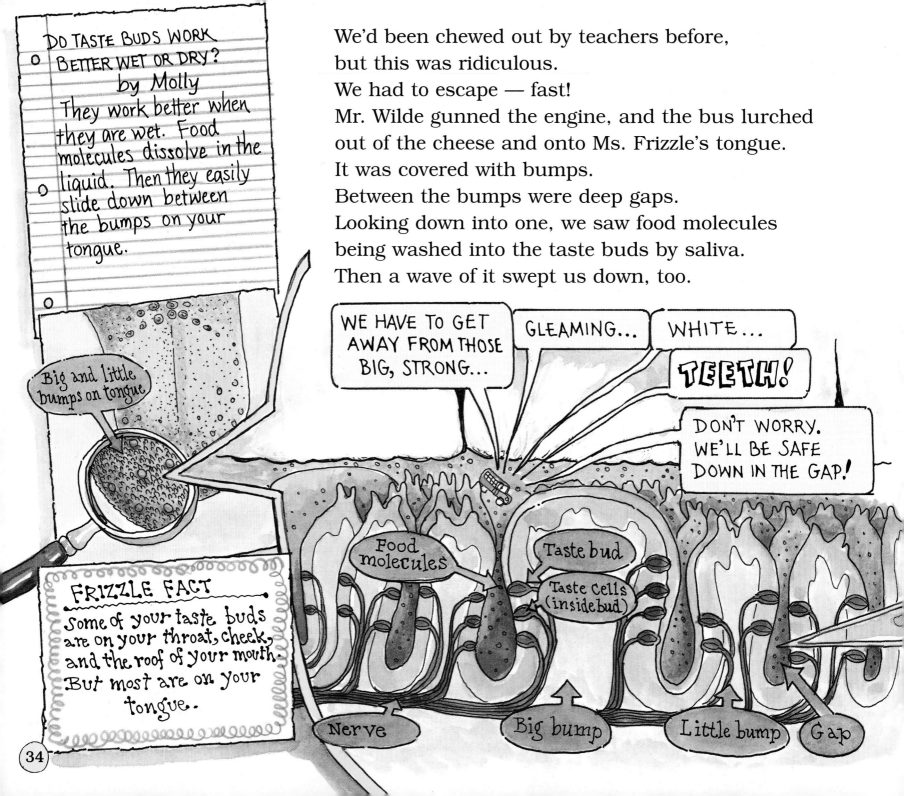

DO TASTE BUDS WORK
BETTER WET OR DRY?
by Molly
They work better when they are wet. Food molecules dissolve in the liquid. Then they easily slide down between the bumps on your tongue.

Big and little bumps on tongue

FRIZZLE FACT
Some of your taste buds are on your throat, cheek, and the roof of your mouth. But most are on your tongue.

We'd been chewed out by teachers before, but this was ridiculous.
We had to escape — fast!
Mr. Wilde gunned the engine, and the bus lurched out of the cheese and onto Ms. Frizzle's tongue.
It was covered with bumps.
Between the bumps were deep gaps.
Looking down into one, we saw food molecules being washed into the taste buds by saliva.
Then a wave of it swept us down, too.

WE HAVE TO GET AWAY FROM THOSE BIG, STRONG...

GLEAMING...

WHITE...

TEETH!

DON'T WORRY. WE'LL BE SAFE DOWN IN THE GAP!

Food molecules

Taste bud

Taste cells (inside bud)

Nerve

Big bump

Little bump

Gap

34

We could have hidden out in the gap
until Ms. Frizzle finished chewing.
But that must have seemed too boring to Mr. Wilde.
He had school-bus fever.
He hung a sharp left into one of the taste buds.
The taste cells inside the bud
were changing the tastes into nerve messages.

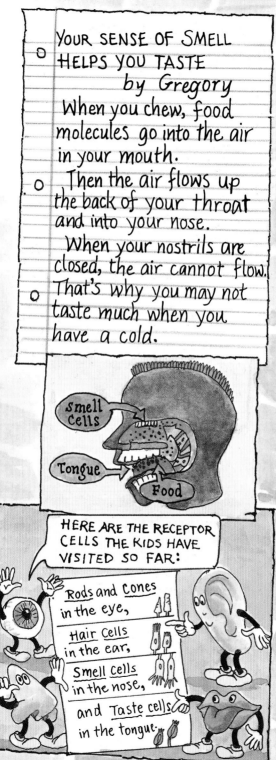

YOUR SENSE OF SMELL
HELPS YOU TASTE
      by Gregory
When you chew, food
molecules go into the air
in your mouth.
   Then the air flows up
the back of your throat
and into your nose.
   When your nostrils are
closed, the air cannot flow.
That's why you may not
taste much when you
have a cold.

Smell cells
Tongue
Food

HERE ARE THE RECEPTOR
CELLS THE KIDS HAVE
VISITED SO FAR:

Rods and Cones
in the eye,
Hair cells
in the ear,
Smell cells
in the nose,
and Taste cells
in the tongue.

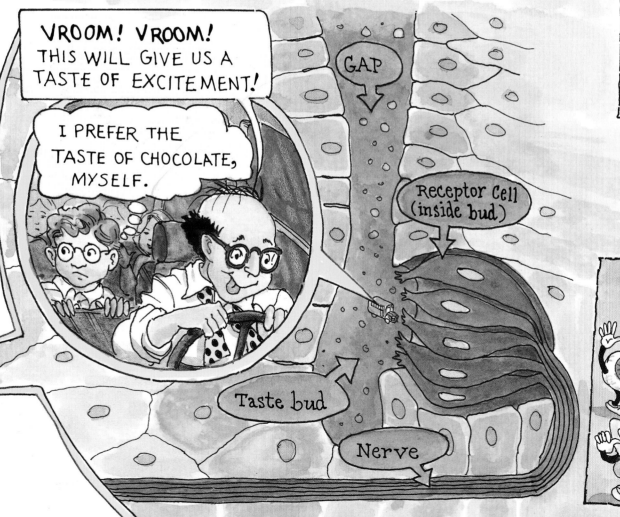

VROOM! VROOM!
THIS WILL GIVE US A
TASTE OF EXCITEMENT!

I PREFER THE
TASTE OF CHOCOLATE,
MYSELF.

GAP

Receptor Cell
(inside bud)

Taste bud

Nerve

HOW MANY FLAVORS CAN YOU TASTE?
by Ralphie

Our taste cells can detect only four tastes: bitter, sour, salty, and sweet. But people can taste over 10,000 different flavors. How is this possible?

IT'S CHOCOLATE!

Scientists say all the flavors we taste are mixtures of the four basic tastes, combined with the many different smells from foods.

FRIZZLE FACT
You can't taste with your mouth alone.
You need your brain, too.

36

Before we knew it, we were traveling on a pathway of nerves to a taste area of Ms. Frizzle's brain. We climbed off the bus and stood on her taste cortex. Now we could taste what our teacher tasted!

WAHOO! IT'S OUR FOURTH VISIT TO A BRAIN.

THIS TIME IT'S MS. FRIZZLE'S BRAIN!!!

UH-OH! THIS COULD BE OUR MOST DANGEROUS TRIP YET!

TASTE CENTER

ANCHOVY

PIZZA

TONGUE

FRIZZLY HAIR

TASTE NERVE

We thought we'd love the taste of Ms. Frizzle's pizza.
But — yuck! — it was covered with *ANCHOVIES!*
We were so grossed out that we ran away
from the taste area of the brain as fast as we could!
Luckily, Mr. Wilde followed us in the bus.

BLAAA-AAH!
THIS PIZZA IS AWFUL!

HASN'T SHE HEARD
OF PEPPERONI?

DON'T TALK —
RUN!

WAIT FOR ME!

ANCHOVIES

Taste sensations

CATFISH WIN THE TASTE
CONTEST
by Wanda
A catfish may have the
most taste buds of any
animal. It has 175,000.
That's about 50 times
as many as the average
human.
Most of the taste buds
are on the <u>outside</u> of
the catfish's body.
It can taste the food
before eating it.

I CAN TASTE
WITH MY BACK
AND MY SIDES
AND MY HEAD.

CHICKENS COME IN LAST
by John
Chickens can taste, but
not very well. They
have only 24
taste buds.

TWENTY-FOUR
IS PLENTY FOR
ME, THANKS.

AFTER ALL,
IT'S ONLY
CHICKEN FEED.

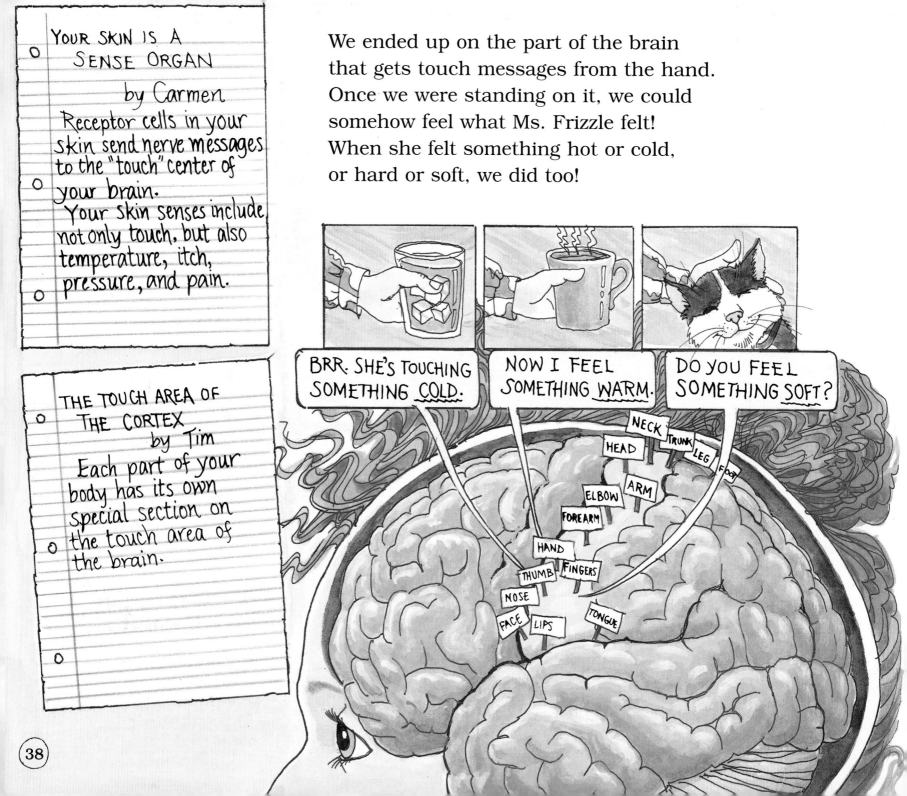

YOUR SKIN IS A
    SENSE ORGAN
        by Carmen
  Receptor cells in your skin send nerve messages to the "touch" center of your brain.
  Your skin senses include, not only touch, but also temperature, itch, pressure, and pain.

THE TOUCH AREA OF
    THE CORTEX
        by Tim
  Each part of your body has its own special section on the touch area of the brain.

We ended up on the part of the brain that gets touch messages from the hand. Once we were standing on it, we could somehow feel what Ms. Frizzle felt! When she felt something hot or cold, or hard or soft, we did too!

BRR. SHE'S TOUCHING SOMETHING <u>COLD.</u>

NOW I FEEL SOMETHING <u>WARM.</u>

DO YOU FEEL SOMETHING <u>SOFT?</u>

NECK
HEAD
TRUNK
LEG
FOOT
ARM
ELBOW
FOREARM
HAND
THUMB
FINGERS
NOSE
FACE
LIPS
TONGUE

"Let's see where this nerve goes," said Mr. Wilde.
Back on the bus, we zoomed along the nerve pathways leading away from Ms. Frizzle's brain.
At the end of the nerves were the receptor cells in her skin.

WE'RE TRAVELING TO MS. FRIZZLE'S SKIN.

IT TAKES A LOT OF NERVE TO GO THERE.

WHISKERS ARE
TOUCH ORGANS
by Shirley

Cats, dogs, mice, horses, and many other mammals have sensitive whiskers.
Whiskers help animals find their way in the dark. A whisker may also detect food that the animal does not see.

WHOA! I ALMOST MISSED THAT ONE!

NOTE: These whiskers are not sense organs.

LOOK AT ALL THE WEIRD RECEPTOR CELLS IN HERE.

Pore

Receptor for vibration

Receptor for heat, itching, and pain

Receptor for Change in shape and extreme cold

ENLARGEMENT OF A SECTION OF SKIN

Receptor for light touch

Sweat gland

Hair follicle receptor

Receptor for deep pressure

39

Q: WHERE IS YOUR SENSE OF BALANCE?
A: IN YOUR EARS!
by Phoebe

In the inner ear, there are three hollow tubes called the semicircular canals.

Hair cells in the canals send messages to your brain about your body's movement.

Then your brain tells your muscles to adjust so your body won't fall.

THE HUMAN EAR

Semicircular Canals are for balance.

Hair cells

Nerve

Cochlea is for hearing.

MIDDLE EAR   INNER EAR

40

"Here's our exit," said Mr. Wilde, driving out through a pore in the skin. Up ahead, we saw the Friz petting her mom's nice soft cat. Mr. Wilde drove so fast that the bus flew right off Ms. Frizzle's hand and into the cat's inner ear.

NOT ANOTHER EAR!

WHAT A CATASTROPHE!

FRED

EARS AREN'T JUST FOR HEARING.

THEY KEEP YOU UPRIGHT, TOO!

RATATAT   RATAT

We passed the snail-shaped cochlea used for hearing.
Then we came to some hollow tubes.
They are used for balancing.
We hung on for dear life as we felt the cat jump.
Next, we heard the rumble of a car engine.
"Seat belts, everyone," yelled Ms. Frizzle, and off we went.

SHALL WE TAKE A RIDE?

GREAT IDEA, VAL. FRED LOVES CARS.

IN MY OLD SCHOOL WE NEVER TRAVELED IN A CAR WHILE WE WERE ON A BUS.

Cochlea

Semicircular canals

INNER EAR OF CAT

A WORD FROM DOROTHY ANN
Semicircular means "shaped like a half-circle."

COOL CATS KEEP THEIR BALANCE   by Tim
Why do cats land on their feet? Their excellent sense of balance helps them turn right side up!
Cat falls--balancing sense says:"You're upside down!"

Head turns

Spine twists--back legs come down

Cat lands on feet

41

SENSATIONAL SENSES
by Rachel

<u>Birds of prey</u> have the best vision in the animal kingdom. An eagle can see eight times better than a person.

Many <u>snakes</u> have sense organs that detect heat. This helps them catch warm-blooded prey.

Heat detectors in special pits in face

<u>Fish</u> have sense cells in lines on the sides of their body. These detect movements in the water.

Lateral line system

This helps fish escape from predators.

When the Friz made a sudden swerve,
we were *cat*apulted out of the ear.
We landed in the road behind Ms. Frizzle's car.
As the bus grew to its regular size again,
Mr. Wilde beeped the horn, and Ms. Frizzle pulled over.

We told her about the meeting, and in no time we were all on our way back to school.

We got there just in time to sing our song
and check out the refreshment table.
Then — what a surprise — Ms. Frizzle got an award.
If anyone deserves an award, it's the Friz.
She's the most *sense*-ational teacher in school!